Original title:
A Snowlit Lantern

Copyright © 2024 Swan Charm
All rights reserved.

Author: Kaido Väinamäe
ISBN HARDBACK: 978-9916-79-339-8
ISBN PAPERBACK: 978-9916-79-340-4
ISBN EBOOK: 978-9916-79-341-1

Radiance Amidst the Flurries

Soft whispers dance in winter's breath,
Golden lights warm the quiet depths.
Amidst the snowflakes' gentle play,
Hope flickers bright, guiding the way.

Every flurry tells a tale,
Of dreams wrapped in a snowy veil.
As stars above wink and gleam,
In the night's embrace, we dare to dream.

Shadows of the Frosted Night

Silent shadows sweep the ground,
In the stillness, peace is found.
Moonlight drapes a silver sheet,
Where frost and cold in darkness meet.

Whispers echo through the trees,
Carried gently by the breeze.
Stars blink out their secrets old,
In the night, a story told.

Glimmering Beacons in the Chill

Tiny lights twinkle in the frost,
Showing paths that were once lost.
Each glimmer shines with hope and grace,
Illuminating this quiet place.

In the chill of winter's grasp,
Warmth in moments we can clasp.
Glimmers dance like fireflies,
In the dark, their magic lies.

Luminescence Beneath the Frost

Underneath the icy sheen,
Life stirs softly, unseen,
Nature holds a whispered light,
In the depths of frosty night.

Amidst the cold that wraps the earth,
Exists a quiet spark of mirth.
Beneath the frost, a heartbeat swells,
In hushed tones, the magic dwells.

Celestial Shadows on Snowy Fields

Under the moon's pale gaze, it glows,
Whispers of winter softly repose.
Footprints etched in fragile white,
Echoes of laughter dance in the night.

Stars peek through the frosted trees,
Carried gently on the chilly breeze.
In every shadow, stories unfold,
Secrets of winter, brave and bold.

Frosty Nobility and Warmth

Glistening crowns on each frozen peak,
Nature's beauty, serene yet unique.
Firewood crackles in the hearth's embrace,
Warmth radiates in this tranquil space.

Majestic beings roam in the night,
Wrapped in a blanket of soft, pure white.
With each breath, the chill finds its home,
Amongst the valleys where winter does roam.

Finding Light in the Silent Snow

Silence blankets the world so wide,
Gentle whispers, winter's guide.
In moments still, the heart can see,
The beauty in simplicity.

With every flake, a story is spun,
As daylight fades, the magic's begun.
Finding solace in the frozen glow,
A dance of peace beneath the snow.

Dappled Glow on a Winter's Eve

Golden hues kiss the twilight sky,
As winter's breath starts to sigh.
Dappled light on the snowflakes play,
Painting warmth at the end of day.

Trees stand tall in their frosty grace,
Holding the secrets of this place.
In the stillness, hearts come alive,
As gentle shadows weave and thrive.

Burst of Light Amidst the Frost

Amidst the chill, a beacon glows,
A shimmer bright in icy clothes.
Whispers dance on winter's breath,
Life ignites beyond the death.

Golden rays break through the gray,
Painting warmth in cold's cruel play.
Branches sparkle like the stars,
A gentle touch, no longer far.

In shadows deep, hope takes flight,
Awakening the heart's delight.
Frosted ground, a canvas wide,
For dreams to bloom, no need to hide.

Gathered warmth in every beam,
A world reborn, a fervent dream.
Nature's pulse, a vibrant song,
Echoes sweet, where we belong.

So let us wander, hand in hand,
Through beauty crafted by time's strand.
A burst of light, in frost we find,
The heart of nature, intertwined.

Radiance of the Quiet Woods

In the stillness, shadows creep,
Where secrets and the quiet seep.
Sunlight filters through the trees,
Awakening the gentle breeze.

Leaves await the morning's grace,
A soft caress, a warm embrace.
With beams of gold, the woods ignite,
A dance of colors, pure delight.

Whispers of the ancients rise,
Echoes soft beneath the skies.
Each branch adorned with hope's embrace,
Radiance found in every space.

In silence, life begins to hum,
A rhythmic pulse, a steady drum.
Nature's song, a soothing balm,
Within the woods, a sacred calm.

So tread lightly on this ground,
In quiet woods, true love is found.
Radiance shines in every hue,
A timeless tale, forever true.

Murmurs of Light in the Frost

In icy grasp, soft whispers glide,
Murmurs sweet where shadows hide.
Gentle light, a fleeting ghost,
A dance of dreams that we love most.

Frosted edges spark and twinkle,
Nature's gems begin to sprinkle.
Each frosty breath, a tiny sigh,
Echoes of life as days go by.

Beneath the frost, the earth takes rest,
Cradled in winter's silken vest.
Mellow hues in twilight blend,
As the light begins to mend.

Rippling streams of silver shine,
In every shadow, stars align.
Murmurs soft, like lullabies,
Awake the heart, as silence sighs.

In frost's embrace, our spirits soar,
A world reborn, forevermore.
With murmurs of light, we find our way,
Through winter's night to greet the day.

Serenity in a World of White

Beneath the blanket, soft and bright,
A world transformed in purest white.
Silence reigns, the heart is still,
In this haven, we find our will.

Snowflakes drift like whispered dreams,
Casting spells in silver beams.
Each flake a wish, the world's delight,
In serene moments, pure and light.

The hush of winter, calm and clear,
Wraps us close, erasing fear.
In this space, we breathe anew,
Finding peace in shades of blue.

Footprints mark this pristine land,
Mapping paths where spirits stand.
A world of white, so soft, so wide,
Invites the soul to take a ride.

So linger in this serene glow,
Let worries fade, let wild thoughts slow.
In a world of white, we find our grace,
Embracing peace in winter's embrace.

Glows of Reflection

In the quiet dusk, shadows play,
Colors dancing, fading away.
Mirrored dreams in the twilight hue,
Whispers of thoughts, softly brew.

Gentle waves on the silver lake,
Nature sighs, in silence awake.
Eager hearts in stillness rest,
Finding peace, their souls are blessed.

Time drifts slow like a drifting leaf,
In every moment, joy and grief.
Echoed whispers of days gone by,
Underneath the vast starlit sky.

Reflections shimmer with soft grace,
In the quiet, we find our place.
Holding dreams like fragile glass,
Each one cherished, hopes amassed.

Twinkling Silence of the Snowfall

Softly falling, the snowflakes glide,
Silent wishes they gently bide.
Blanketing whispers on frozen ground,
In this hush, serenity found.

Tree branches hold their frosted dreams,
Under moonlight, everything gleams.
A world transformed in purest white,
The beauty lies in silent night.

Footsteps muffled beneath the snow,
As time takes pause, and hearts grow slow.
Every flake tells a tale of peace,
In the cold, all worries cease.

Twinkling stars peep down from above,
In the stillness, we feel the love.
Each breath a cloud in the chilly air,
Wrapped in beauty, without a care.

The Soft Glimmer of Hope

In the shadows, a light appears,
Whispers of dreams chase off the fears.
Softly glowing, a spark so bright,
Illuminating the darkest night.

Hearts united in warm embrace,
Against the odds, we find our place.
Through every challenge, we hold tight,
With the glimmer, we ignite.

Moments frail, yet filled with grace,
In the chaos, we find our space.
Each heartbeat echoes the strength we share,
A gentle promise, we're always there.

When storms rage and shadows deepen,
Hope's soft glow is ever steepin'.
Together we rise, never alone,
In every heart, a spark is sown.

Beacons Beneath the Ice

Beneath the ice, a fire burns bright,
Hidden warmth in the cold of night.
Echoes of life in the frozen layer,
Whispers of hope that dance like prayer.

Delicate roots reach for the sun,
In darkened depths, life's never done.
Through crystal coatings, bright and clear,
Resilience thrives, ever near.

Silent stories of strength unfold,
In icy chambers, brave and bold.
Each heartbeat a lighthouse in freeze,
Guiding us through life's rugged seas.

Emerging from winter's tight embrace,
We seek the warmth in love's sweet grace.
Together we stand, side by side,
Beacons of hope, our hearts the guide.

Shimmering Shadows

In the dusk, shadows dance,
Whispers of a twilight chance.
Moonlight drapes on ancient trees,
Softly swaying in the breeze.

Secrets linger in the dark,
Fleeting glimmers, tiny spark.
Night unfolds her velvet shade,
Memories in twilight made.

Stars peek through the velvet veil,
Tales of love and hope to sail.
Each shadow has a story told,
In their depths, a heart of gold.

Eclipsed by dreams yet to flow,
In the quiet, feelings grow.
Shimmering whispers, soft and bright,
Filling hearts with ethereal light.

The night, a canvas, dark and wide,
Where shimmering shadows coincide.
In their depths, we find our way,
Guided by the stars' ballet.

The Glow of Quiet Nights

Stars above in silence gleam,
Night enfolds us in a dream.
Flickering lights in the deep blue,
Softly whispering, 'I love you.'

The moon bathes all in silver glow,
Casting shadows soft and slow.
In stillness, time seems to freeze,
Wrapped in warmth, a gentle breeze.

Crickets serenade the hour,
Nature's music, subtle power.
Each heartbeat feels like a song,
In this peace, we both belong.

The world outside fades away,
In your arms, I long to stay.
Every moment shines so bright,
Bathed in the glow of quiet night.

Softly, dreams begin to weave,
In this magic, we believe.
Together, under starlit skies,
The glow of love never dies.

Winter's Gentle Embrace

Snowflakes fall in a silent dance,
Covering earth in a soft expanse.
The world dressed in white so pure,
In winter's arms, we feel secure.

Fires crackle, warmth does ignite,
Cocooned in blankets, sweet delight.
Outside, cold winds softly sigh,
Inside, dreams drift, and spirits fly.

Footprints trace where love has gone,
Underneath the glowing dawn.
Winter's chill, a tender call,
In its embrace, we share it all.

Icicles shimmer, catching light,
Sparkling jewels, a wondrous sight.
Nature sleeps, calm and serene,
In this stillness, peace is seen.

As the world rests, hearts entwine,
Winter's touch, a love divine.
In its gentle, soft caress,
We find warmth in winter's dress.

A Radiant Solstice

As daylight lingers, skies aglow,
Nature's beauty starts to show.
Solstice whispers, warm and bright,
Encircling us in soft sunlight.

Golden rays through leaves cascade,
In each moment, memories made.
Time stands still as shadows play,
In this magic, we find our way.

Gathered around the glowing fire,
Connecting hearts, igniting desire.
Stories shared beneath the stars,
In this night, our dreams are ours.

Every heartbeat, every glance,
Echoes of a fateful chance.
In the warmth of summer's grace,
We bask in love's sweet embrace.

A radiant solstice, bright and clear,
Filling our souls with cheer.
In nature's glow, we feel alive,
Together, forever we thrive.

Navigation by the Frosted Flame

In the glow of the frosted flame,
We wander paths, never the same.
The winter's breath whispers near,
Guiding hearts, calming fear.

Stars above in silent flight,
Twinkling gems in the deep night.
Each step brings warmth, pure delight,
In shadows deep, there's guiding light.

Branches sway, dressed in white,
Where dreams take wing, taking flight.
A lantern bright, our truest aim,
Through the dark, we stake our claim.

Frosted whispers weave our tale,
Through frozen paths, we shall prevail.
With each flicker, hope is borne,
In a world reborn each dawn.

So gather 'round, let spirits lift,
In frosted flame, our loving gift.
Together we chart the unseen way,
Navigating night to greet the day.

Veils of Light in a Frozen Realm

Veils of light dance, shimmering bright,
In the frozen realm, a wondrous sight.
Each twirl of snow, an elegant grace,
Brings warmth to this cold embrace.

Whispers of winter in the air,
Glimmers of magic everywhere.
With every breath, a spark ignites,
Healing souls in the frosty nights.

Beneath the dark, the soft glow glides,
Carving dreams in the snowy tides.
A hush falls over the world so wide,
As hope emerges, our hearts collide.

Through crystalline paths, we'll roam and gleam,
With veils of light, we rise and dream.
In the cold embrace, we find our place,
In this frozen realm, love interlace.

Together we'll weave the tales of old,
In the warmth of light, our spirits bold.
Through veils of light, we shall explore,
In this frozen realm, forevermore.

Threads of Illumination in Winter's Grasp

Threads of light in winter's grasp,
Entwined with dreams, an endless clasp.
In the chill, a spark ignites,
Filling hearts with warm delights.

Snowflakes fall, like whispered prayer,
Gentle touch in the chilled air.
Each moment glows, a timely please,
A dance of warmth amidst the freeze.

We trace the stars on frosty nights,
Guided by soft and twinkling lights.
In this realm where silence sleeps,
The promise of spring quietly creeps.

With every step, our spirits soar,
Unraveling threads, we seek for more.
In winter's grasp, we find our way,
Illuminated paths, come what may.

So gather close, through cold we chase,
Threads of hope in a loving space.
In winter's hold, our hearts will sing,
With threads of light, we welcome spring.

Glimmers in the Frost

Beneath the moon's soft glow,
The world is draped in white.
Each crystal sparkles bright,
A beautiful, pure sight.

The branches bow with grace,
Adorned with icy lace.
In silence, dreams take flight,
In this enchanting night.

Footsteps crunch on the ground,
Nature's whisper is found.
In every twinkling shard,
A secret, softly starred.

The breath of winter cold,
Wraps the earth in its hold.
A stillness all around,
Where peace is truly found.

With every fleeting glint,
The heart begins to sprint.
For in the frosty air,
Magic lingers everywhere.

Whispers of the Winter Light

In the early morning's gleam,
Soft whispers fill the air.
The frosts like diamonds beam,
A tender, fragile flair.

The sun peeks o'er the hill,
Crafting shadows so bold.
Its warmth begins to thrill,
As winter's tale unfolds.

Each flake that softly falls,
Tells stories from the sky.
In silence, nature calls,
And time begins to fly.

Crisp air, alive, refined,
Brings memories anew.
In every gust we find,
The promise of the blue.

The day, a canvas bright,
Awakens with delight.
In whispers soft and light,
Winter's grace takes flight.

Radiance on the White Path

Along the snowy trail,
Where whispers of dreams soar.
Each footstep tells a tale,
Of journeys we explore.

The sun reflects like gold,
On snow so pure and bright.
A warmth within the cold,
Guiding us through the night.

Winds weave through the trees,
A chorus, wild and free.
In every gentle breeze,
Whispers call out to me.

The path sings with delight,
As stars begin to twinkle.
In shadows and in light,
The heart starts to crinkle.

With every step we take,
Radiance gently glows.
On this path, love we make,
As winter's magic flows.

Beacon in the Frozen Night

A beacon bright and bold,
Stands against the night's chill.
Its warmth, a story told,
A guide through winter's thrill.

The stars in silence watch,
As shadows dance and play.
The moon, a silver blotch,
Leads wandering souls astray.

In the quiet, we seek,
A spark amid the frost.
Through echoes, whispers speak,
Of all that we have lost.

Yet hope, like embers glow,
In hearts prepared to blaze.
A light that starts to grow,
In this frozen maze.

Together we will find,
The warmth that brings us near.
A beacon intertwined,
With love, we hold so dear.

Gleaming Hopes in the Dark

In shadows deep where whispers dwell,
A flicker stirs, a secret swell.
Each heartbeat held and softly framed,
A beacon bright, hope unashamed.

Through midnight trails, we wander bold,
With every step, new dreams unfold.
The dark may rise, but light will gleam,
In the silence, we dare to dream.

The nightingale sings, a gentle sound,
In hidden glades where joys abound.
With every note, the fears retreat,
A symphony where hearts can meet.

So let the hopes like fireflies dance,
In twilight's grasp, we find our chance.
For in the night, we hold the key,
To open paths and set us free.

The Lantern's Soliloquy in a Snow-Wrapped World

In frosted air, a lantern glows,
Its amber warmth, a tale it knows.
The snowflakes fall, a soft ballet,
Embracing light in twilight's play.

Each flicker speaks of dreams untold,
Of laughter shared, of hearts so bold.
It whispers secrets in the night,
A guiding star, a gentle light.

Through winter's chill, it stands alone,
A steadfast heart, a message known.
To those who seek a path unsealed,
With hope and love, their fate revealed.

In every gust, the stories sway,
Of warmth and joy in disarray.
The world may freeze, yet still it beams,
A beacon bright, igniting dreams.

Soft Glow of the Winter Moon

Beneath the night, the winter moon,
A soft embrace, a silver tune.
It bathes the world in gentle hues,
While whispered winds sing lullabies true.

In snowy fields, the shadows creep,
As dreams arise from silent sleep.
The moon, a watchful guardian,
Keeps solitude so warm, so drawn.

Each glimmer tells a story spun,
Of stars above, and journeys begun.
With every phase, a change we find,
A cycle eternal, sweet and kind.

The night unfolds its velvet cloak,
In this stillness, our hearts evoke.
The winter moon, a soft retreat,
A place where peace and magic meet.

Hearth's Embrace in a Frigid Landscape

Amidst the snow, the hearth abides,
Where warmth and safety gently guides.
The crackling flames, a dance of light,
In winter's grasp, they hold us tight.

With every log, a memory gleams,
Of laughter shared and woven dreams.
In shadows cast, our stories blend,
As time unwinds, we find our mend.

The chill may bite, the winds may wail,
But here within, love will prevail.
Each heartbeat felt, each gaze we share,
In hearth's embrace, we shed our care.

Thus winter's chill may roam outside,
Yet in this space, we'll bide and glide.
For warmth ignites when hearts align,
In frigid lands, forever shine.

Twilight Glow on Winter Trails

The sun sinks low in evening's grace,
A soft glow warms the frosty space.
Footprints lead through powdery white,
Nature holds its breath, in twilight light.

Whispers of wind in branches play,
As shadows dance and softly sway.
Golden hues on snowflakes gleam,
The world a part of a tranquil dream.

Sparkling crystals in the air,
Each step taken, free from care.
With every breath, the chill brings cheer,
In this stillness, our hearts steer.

A silent path beneath the trees,
The night awakens, calm as the seas.
Stars emerge, a blanket of light,
Guiding us through the peaceful night.

Echoes of Warmth in Winter's Embrace

Fires flicker in the cozy den,
Holding warmth, where dreams begin.
Laughter rings through the frosty air,
Togetherness, a bond we share.

Blankets wrapped in gentle folds,
Stories shared, as the night unfolds.
The chill outside is no match for
The warmth within, our spirits soar.

Cups of cocoa, steam rising high,
Glimmers of joy in every sigh.
Outside the world is pure and white,
But love's embrace keeps us tight.

Each spark of fire, a memory made,
In every heart, the warmth cascades.
Through winter nights, we find our way,
Echoes of love that forever stay.

Guiding Light Through the Snowy Fog

Fog rolls in on quiet feet,
Whispers soft, a blanket fleet.
A lantern glows, its light shines bright,
Leading us through the velvet night.

Snowflakes dance like dreams untold,
A silent world, so quiet and bold.
With every step, the shadows blend,
In this stillness, our worries mend.

Branches heavy with winter's lace,
Nature's artistry, a perfect place.
The soft crunch underfoot sings clear,
A melody only we can hear.

Guiding us through the misty veil,
Each turn taken, we will prevail.
Together we walk, hand in hand,
In this magic, forever we stand.

Aurora of Light in a Winter Night

The sky ignites with colors bright,
A dance of dreams, pure delight.
Beneath the stars, a canvas spun,
Nature's masterpiece has begun.

In hues of green and violet sway,
The heavens below, a bright display.
Ribbons of light in the cold night air,
Whispers of beauty, everywhere.

As shadows stretch across the land,
We stand in wonder, hand in hand.
A moment frozen in pure gaze,
A fleeting glimpse of winter's praise.

The aurora dances, wild and free,
Capturing hearts in harmony.
In this wonder, we find our flight,
In the aurora of a winter night.

Shards of Light in the Night

In shadows deep, the stars ignite,
A silver glow breaks through the night.
Each shard of light, a whispered dream,
Reflecting hopes, a gentle beam.

They dance across the waiting sea,
In fleeting moments, wild and free.
A tapestry of night and grace,
Eternal warmth in a cold space.

Flickers shine where darkness reigns,
Softening edges, easing pains.
In darkest hours, they guide our way,
Leading hearts 'til dawn's first ray.

With every pulse, the cosmos gleams,
Awakening forgotten dreams.
A melody of starlit sighs,
In the vastness of endless skies.

So let us wander through the shades,
Where starlit paths and hope cascades.
With shards of light, our souls unite,
In whispers shared, through endless night.

The Dance of Winter's Light

Beneath the snow, the earth holds still,
As winter wraps its heart in chill.
A dance of frost, in silence bright,
The world transformed by winter's light.

Dancing shadows, crisp and clear,
Whirling whispers, drawing near.
Each flake a note in nature's song,
In this embrace, we all belong.

The twilight glimmers, soft and wide,
A silver thread where dreams abide.
As night descends, the stars alight,
Inviting us to share their flight.

The moon reflects on icy streams,
Awakening our deepest dreams.
In every breath, a spark ignites,
A symphony of winter nights.

Let us embrace the quiet grace,
Of winter's dance, its tender space.
With every step, we find delight,
In the soft glow of winter's light.

Whispers in the Cold Dawn

The dawn breaks soft, the world is still,
Embraced by quiet, tranquil thrill.
Whispers weave through frosty air,
A fragile touch, a silent prayer.

Each blade of grass, a sparkling gem,
Awakens life from night's diadem.
A canvas brushed in hues so bright,
Painting hope with morning's light.

The chill retreats, the warmth arrives,
In gentle strokes, the dawn revives.
Birds take flight, on wings of cheer,
Their melodies, the heart will hear.

In every sigh, the world renews,
As whispers dance with morning's hues.
A tapestry of life unfolds,
In stories whispered, softly told.

So let us greet this brand new day,
With open hearts, and joy in sway.
For in the chill, we find our way,
In whispers of the cold dawn's play.

Light's Tender Breathe on Snow

The snowflakes fall, a soft embrace,
Each crystal holds a fleeting grace.
Light wraps around, a gentle glow,
A tender breathe on winter's snow.

Each step we take, a whispered sound,
Echoes softly, the world profound.
In quiet moments, we reflect,
On love and peace, so deep, so etched.

The trees adorned with shimmering white,
Stand tall and proud, a stunning sight.
With every flake, a story spun,
Of light and dark, of lost and won.

As night descends, the stars will gleam,
In this stillness, we dare to dream.
For in the cold, our hearts ignite,
With warmth and hope, a guiding light.

So let us bask in winter's glow,
And cherish all that the season shows.
For in the hush, we find our way,
In light's tender breathe on snow's display.

Resplendent Winter Hues

Snowflakes dance on brisk air,
Painting whispers in the night.
Pines wear coats of crystal white,
The world shimmers, pure and fair.

Frosted branches, nature's lace,
Glimmering under pale moonlight.
In this hush, we find our place,
Every shadow a soft sight.

Cold winds carry tales of peace,
As dawn breaks with blushing grace.
Winter's beauty will not cease,
In silence, we find embrace.

Icicles hang like delicate jewels,
Reflecting dreams in dawn's embrace.
Nature's canvas with vibrant hues,
Awakens hearts to winter's pace.

The air is crisp with stories told,
Beneath a quilt of silver sleep.
In the warmth of memories bold,
Resplendent joys we tenderly keep.

The Light of Untold Stories

In shadows deep, the stories wait,
Lost whispers beckon to be heard.
Each moment holds a twist of fate,
Unraveled gently, word by word.

Dusty tomes upon the shelf,
Secrets in the quiet night.
Voices echo, tales of self,
Illuminating hidden light.

Through windows cracked, the breezes swirl,
Carrying hopes like autumn leaves.
In every silence, dreams unfurl,
Awaiting hearts the truth receives.

Beyond the mystic veil we chase,
Timid hands reach for the flame.
In the heart, we find our place,
Bathed in glow and timeless name.

Remembered lore from days of yore,
Spinning webs of olden dreams.
In the light, forevermore,
Stories bind us at the seams.

Frosty Fragments of Light

Dewdrops catch the early sun,
Fragments dance upon the grass.
In frozen breath, the day's begun,
Nature's sigh, a world to pass.

Skies of lavender and gold,
Curtains drawn on winter's play.
Wonders shyly, still and bold,
Echo through the crisp decay.

Whispers of the frost entice,
Every glimmer begs to stay.
Life renews with soft advice,
Chill and warmth intertwine the way.

From icy firs, the light cascades,
Painting shadows, sharp and clear.
In the stillness, joy parades,
Fragments glisten, drawing near.

In every crystal gaze we seek,
The essence of what once was light.
Frosty tales begin to speak,
Beneath the stars, a sweet delight.

Illuminating the Stillness

Amid the snow, a tranquil hush,
Time flows gently, quiet grace.
In every whispered, icy rush,
We find solace, a warm embrace.

Moonlight shines on tranquil streams,
Reflecting secrets softly kept.
In the silence, lingered dreams,
Awake where shadows adept.

Stars murmur in the calm of night,
Guiding lost hearts on their way.
In the cosmos, distant light,
Illuminates the path we sway.

Each breath taken in this space,
Provides wisdom, tender and steep.
A moment caught, a sacred place,
In stillness, we find what we reap.

Here, nature speaks in gentle tones,
Inviting us to slow our pace.
In every heart, a quiet home,
Illuminating love's embrace.

Frosted Corners of the Mind

In the hush of winter's breath,
Thoughts gather like fragile snow,
Whispers of dreams long forgotten,
Laying soft on the heart's warm glow.

Shadows dance, bright against white,
Memories cling like frost on glass,
Each sparkle a shard of the past,
Echoes of moments that swiftly pass.

Time drips slowly, like melting ice,
Revealing the warmth hidden beneath,
Each heartbeat a candle flickering,
A beacon where silence does wreathe.

Fingers trace paths in the chill,
Carving the stories we hold dear,
Frosted corners shelter the light,
Guiding us through shadow and fear.

In stillness, the mind takes flight,
To places where the heart finds peace,
Lost in the frost, we are found,
In whispers, our worries cease.

Candlelight in a Winter's Dream

The glow of a flame in the dark,
Dancing shadows on the wall,
Warmth wraps around like a cloak,
Inviting us to let ourselves fall.

Candles flicker, secrets they share,
A story whispered from the night,
With each movement, a spark appears,
Creating a world of soft light.

Outside, snow blankets the ground,
While inside, we find sweet reprieve,
In the stillness of winter's dream,
Hope glimmers through what we believe.

The air carries scents of pine,
Mixed with a hint of sweet spice,
Moments suspended in time,
Embracing the warmth that feels so nice.

Together we sit, hearts entwined,
Under the spell of this night's gleam,
Candlelight flickers, love ignites,
In the magic of winter's dream.

Cold Glow of Serenity

Underneath a canopy of stars,
A hush blankets the sleeping earth,
Cold glow casts peace over all,
In the darkness, we find rebirth.

Moonlight dances on frozen lakes,
Whispers of stillness fill the air,
Silent symphonies play for the soul,
As hearts bare their burdens and care.

Breath hangs lightly, a frosty mist,
Each exhale a wish to the skies,
Serenity found in quietude,
Where worries dissolve and hope lies.

Frosted branches, a delicate lace,
Cradling secrets only they know,
In their stillness, a wisdom resides,
Holding the stories of all who flow.

We wander through this tranquil night,
With dreams woven in the starlight,
In the cold glow of serene grace,
Our spirits take wing, pure and bright.

Lanterns of the Longest Night

Lanterns flicker in the deep,
Guiding the lost along their way,
Each one a story to uncover,
In the heart of the longest day.

Shadows stretch down narrow streets,
Whispers ride the chill of the night,
Through the cold, we search for warmth,
As lanterns cast their gentle light.

The world slows to a thoughtful pause,
While the stars begin to unfold,
Each twinkle a promise held tight,
Wrapped in the glow, brave and bold.

In the distance, echoes of laughter,
Mingle with the soft winter air,
CLOSE the doors to the worries outside,
Find comfort in those who care.

We gather, hearts alight with dreams,
As lanterns illuminate our souls,
In the longest night, we find strength,
Together, we make the shadows whole.

Frosted Dreams and Nighttime Gleams

In quiet nights, the world does sleep,
With frosted dreams that softly creep.
Stars above, like diamonds gleam,
Whispering wishes, a gentle theme.

Under the moon's serene embrace,
The snowflakes dance, a tender grace.
Voices soft, in the icy air,
A lullaby of dreams laid bare.

Silent shadows, shadows play,
As winter's chill begins to sway.
In frosted hues, all things align,
Nature's beauty, purely divine.

The world transformed, a sparkling sight,
With every breath, a frosty bite.
In the stillness, hope takes flight,
Dreams illuminated by the night.

In the heart of winter's glow,
A warmth that only we can know.
In the frosted dreams, we find our way,
Guided gently until the break of day.

Illuminated Whispers of Winter

Whispers carried on icy winds,
The beauty of winter never ends.
Street lamps glow with golden light,
Illuminating paths of sheer delight.

Softly falling, snowflakes sway,
Dressing the earth in white array.
In the silence, a story unfolds,
As nature's magic gently holds.

Each breath is seen in frosty air,
Moments cherished, beyond compare.
Underneath the chilly dome,
Winter sings of love and home.

The trees shimmer with diamonds bright,
Guardians of this starry night.
In every shadow, spirits roam,
Illuminated whispers find their home.

A tapestry of winter's gleam,
Stitching dreams into a seam.
Within the chilled embrace, we know,
Warmth ignites through winter's glow.

Glistening Pathways Through the Snow

Footsteps track the path of white,
Glistening softly in the night.
Every step, a story told,
In sparkling crystals, brave and bold.

Through frosty woods, the silence hums,
Where beauty beckons, nature drums.
Trees adorned in cloaks of ice,
A glistening world, a paradise.

With every breath, the cold invites,
A dance of shadows, playful sights.
Moonlit paths, a sight to savor,
Leading onwards, a soulful favor.

Snowflakes swirl in rhythmic grace,
Kissing cheeks, a tender embrace.
In the hush, the heartbeats sing,
Embracing all that winter brings.

Each glistening path whispers so sweet,
In winter's hold, our spirits meet.
Through snowy trails, we joyfully roam,
Finding magic, we are home.

Enchantment of the Frosted Glow

In twilight's hush, a world adorned,
With frost and light, the night is warmed.
Candles flicker, shadows play,
In a landscape where dreams hold sway.

The frosted glow, a soft caress,
Wrapping the earth in its finesse.
Gentle whispers from the trees,
In the winter's breath, we find our ease.

A canvas white, under the moon,
Stars twinkle softly, nature's tune.
In the stillness, hearts align,
In this enchantment, we entwine.

With every turn, the beauty grows,
In winter's festival, magic flows.
An orchestra of peace unfolds,
Tales of wonder, quietly told.

So let us dance in frost's embrace,
In every moment, find our grace.
Through the night, our spirits glow,
In the enchantment of the frosted glow.

Luminescent Dreams in Snow

In silence falls the soft white glow,
A canvas pure, where dreams can flow.
Each flake a star from night above,
Whispers of wonder, dreams of love.

Footprints trace a path so neat,
In the stillness, heartbeats meet.
The world transforms, a gentle sigh,
As snowflakes dance from the cloudy sky.

Luminous hues in twilight gleam,
Painting scenes from a silent dream.
In the distance, shadows play,
Embracing night, surrendering day.

Beneath the moon's soft silver light,
Hope glimmers in the quiet night.
Each breath a wish, a promise made,
In this realm, fears slowly fade.

Awakened hearts, the spirit yearns,
For warmth in the cold, the fire burns.
In luminescent dreams we find,
The magic born of heart and mind.

Glowing in the Heart of Winter

Amidst the frost, a fire ignites,
With every breath, the warmth ignites.
The chill surrounds but hearts grow bright,
In winter's grasp, we find our light.

Crisp air carries laughter bold,
Fireside tales of days of old.
In the heart of winter, hope remains,
Bound by love, despite the chains.

Beneath the stars, the world is still,
Each moment savored, time to thrill.
A glowing ember in the night,
Illuminates the path of light.

Snowflakes twirl in playful dance,
Nature's beauty, a fleeting chance.
Embrace the cold, let spirits soar,
In winter's heart, find something more.

When shadows stretch and daylight wanes,
Hold close the warmth, forget the pains.
In glowing embers, dreams ignite,
A tapestry of love and light.

Frosty Whispers of Radiance

The dawn arrives, a frosty breath,
Beneath the ice, life knows no death.
Whispers echo through the trees,
Sweet serenades upon the breeze.

In every flake, a story spun,
Of winter nights and morning sun.
Sparkling jewels on branches lie,
A crystal world beneath the sky.

Shadows dance in morning's grace,
Painting scenes in a soft embrace.
Frosty glimmers, pure and bright,
Radiant dreams that take to flight.

As sunlight breaks the coldest realm,
The heart finds warmth, begins to helm.
In nature's splendor, we discover,
The frosty whispers of each other.

Resilient hearts, we rise anew,
In winter's chill, our love shines through.
With every gaze, find beauty near,
Frosty whispers, forever clear.

Silhouettes of a Silver Dawn

As daylight breaks with silvery hues,
A dance of shadows, the heart renews.
Figures emerge from the night's embrace,
Carved in light, in a tranquil space.

Beneath the boughs, where secrets hide,
A world awaits, with arms open wide.
Silhouettes whisper of journeys bold,
Stories of warmth in the winter's cold.

Snow blankets ground in pristine white,
Every contour kissed by light.
In this silence, spirits swell,
Echoing hopes that time will tell.

Silver glimmers on the icy streams,
Reflecting back our silent dreams.
Awakening hearts, we rise to see,
The dawn of warmth, sweet harmony.

Each moment glows, a perfect frame,
Life unfolds, we're not the same.
In silhouettes of dawn so bright,
We find our home, our love, our light.

Celestial Glow of Nighttime

Stars twinkle bright in the sky,
Whispers of dreams drift way up high.
Moonlit beams dance on the ground,
In the quiet, magic is found.

Clouds softly float like cotton candy,
The night is calm, yet so uncanny.
Each shadow tells a story sweet,
Under the glow, our hearts do meet.

Gentle winds carry a tune,
As crickets sing to the bright moon.
The world below rests in peace,
While the nighttime wonders increase.

Through the stillness, secrets unfold,
In whispers of starlight bold.
Nature's blanket, so vast and deep,
Invites us all to dream, to leap.

With every gaze, horizons glow,
In the celestial night's gentle show.
Awakened hearts beneath the dome,
In the night sky, we find our home.

The Frost's Embrace of Illumination

Morning light kisses icy breath,
Frosty whispers defy the death.
Crystals glisten on branches bare,
Nature's artwork, a beauty rare.

Sunrise breaks through winter's clutch,
Soft hues painting the world as such.
Every shimmer a fleeting glance,
In the cold, life finds its dance.

Air so crisp, each breath a sigh,
Under the blue of the wide sky.
A sharp chill bites but warms the soul,
Within the frost, we are made whole.

Glow of day battles night's retreat,
With each moment, the two shades meet.
In this embrace, we find our way,
Guided by light through the fray.

As dusk arrives, the chill takes hold,
Stars emerge in a story told.
Wrapped in frost, we seek the light,
In its warmth, we find our flight.

Echoes of Soft Radiance

In twilight's hush, echoes arise,
Soft radiance fills the dusky skies.
Whispers of light flicker and sway,
Guiding us gently on our way.

Across the fields, the glow does play,
Unraveling secrets of the day.
Each shadow casts a mystic spell,
In this twilight, all is well.

Candles flicker in windows near,
Hearts unite, we hold them dear.
Each laugh and whisper, a melody,
In the soft glow, we are free.

The world transforms in hues so bright,
In this gentle embrace of light.
Fading echo of the setting sun,
In stillness, we find we are one.

Soft radiance, a calming balm,
Wraps the night in a quilt of calm.
Through echoes, old stories revive,
In this gentle glow, we thrive.

Lanterns Along a Glistening Path

Lanterns bobbing in the night air,
Illuminate dreams, dispel despair.
Each flicker leads where shadows breathe,
On this path, our wishes seethe.

Glistening stones beneath our feet,
Guide our steps with a rhythm sweet.
Through the trees, their glow entwines,
Every heart finds where it aligns.

The journey unfolds, hearts alive,
In the glow, we learn to thrive.
With every step, stories unfold,
In whispers of joy, our dreams bold.

Through paths of light, we wander free,
Each lantern beckoning you and me.
In this dance, time slips away,
Together, we find our way.

As night descends, the lanterns sway,
Leading us homeward, come what may.
In their embrace, we're never lost,
For love's light shines, no matter the cost.

Glows and Shadows of Frosted Evenings

In the quiet dusk, the glow ignites,
Soft whispers beckon, in fading light.
Frosted breath lingers, a silent shroud,
Casting dreams where the shadows crowd.

Twilight dances on icy streams,
As stars emerge to weave our dreams.
Each glimmer holds a secret past,
In the night's embrace, we are steadfast.

Trees stand sentinel, bathed in white,
Framed by the night and silvered light.
Footsteps crunch on the frozen ground,
In this stillness, peace is found.

The glow from windows flickers near,
Drawing us close, inviting cheer.
Moments linger, the world feels small,
In the warmth of love, we embrace it all.

As frost weaves lace on the window pane,
Our hearts unite, free from pain.
Glows and shadows, a dance so sweet,
In frosted evenings, our souls meet.

Light Dancing on Snowflakes

A sparkling flurry dances in air,
Each flake unique, beyond compare.
Sunlight weaves through the icy fray,
Painting the world in a shimmering play.

As winter whispers with soft delight,
The snowflakes twirl in purest light.
Glistening wonders from heaven's space,
Caught in joy, a moment's grace.

Children laugh as they spin and twirl,
Fingers outstretched, in a flurry swirl.
The magic sparkles, igniting the day,
With whispers of wonder that always stay.

Nature's canvas, a picture bright,
Illuminated softly, a pure delight.
Each snowflake's descent, a gentle kiss,
Reminds us of beauty, filled with bliss.

With every heartbeat, the light expands,
Guiding us through winter's lands.
A dance of joy beneath the sky,
As light twirls, and snowflakes fly.

Illuminated Pathways Through the Winter Wood

In winter's hold, the pathways gleam,
Lined with whispers of a silver dream.
Tall trees stand watch, their branches bare,
Beneath the moonlight's tender care.

Footprints crunch on powdered snow,
Leading us where soft breezes blow.
Each step draws near to nature's heart,
A tranquil journey, a work of art.

Stars above in their shimmering choir,
Fill the night with a warmth like fire.
Paths illuminated by dreams untold,
Guiding us gently through the cold.

Echoes of woodland tunes take flight,
While shadows dance in soft twilight.
With every turn, a mystery reveals,
The magic hidden in winter's seals.

Beyond the boughs, a world anew,
Painted in hues of frosted blue.
Illuminated pathways lead the way,
In winter woods where dreams lay.

Lunar Dreams in the Winter Chill

Beneath the moon, the night is still,
Crickets hush in the winter chill.
Lunar glow caresses the snow,
Whispers secrets that softly flow.

Dreams take flight on the frosty air,
Guided by stars, a cosmic glare.
Silver beams dance on sculpted white,
Encapsulating the stillness of night.

A gentle hush, the world asleep,
In lunar dreams, our visions seep.
Time stands still, wrapped in delight,
As hopes awaken in starry light.

Crystalline branches shimmer bright,
Cradled in warmth of a moonlit night.
Each breath brings forth a quiet wish,
Dancing with stars in celestial bliss.

In winter's chill, we find our way,
Guided by dreams that softly sway.
Lunar enchantments, wrapped in grace,
Whisper of magic time can't erase.

Chasing Light in Icy Silence

In the hush of winter's breath,
Shadows dance, they weave and wreathe.
Whispers echo through the night,
Chasing dreams in icy light.

Footprints trace a fragile path,
Through the snow, a gentle math.
Sparkling stars watch from above,
Guiding hearts with silent love.

A crystal breeze begins to sigh,
As the troubled thoughts drift by.
In the stillness, hope ignites,
Chasing light through frosty nights.

The moon casts silver on the ground,
With each heartbeat, solace found.
Nature's peace a soothing balm,
In this calm, I feel so calm.

Embers glow in distant dreams,
Filling voids with radiant beams.
As I venture through the cold,
Chasing light, brave and bold.

Lanterns of the Arctic Night

In the stillness of the night,
Lanterns glow with gentle light.
Flickering softly, guiding hands,
Through the dark, where silence stands.

Above, the stars twinkle bright,
Symbols of hope in the night.
Through the frost, shadows play,
Chasing dreams that drift away.

Icy winds sing lullabies,
Wrapped in warmth, beneath the skies.
Every breath, a fleeting chance,
Underneath the moonlit dance.

Softened whispers in the air,
Embracing all without a care.
Wandering hearts find their way,
Guided by lanterns' sway.

In the arctic's hush, I stand,
Feeling magic in this land.
With each flicker, stories soar,
Lanterns of light forevermore.

Shining Solitude Under the Stars

Solitude in starlit skies,
Where a thousand wishes rise.
Each twinkle, a story told,
In the night, I feel so bold.

Lost in dreams of endless space,
Finding solace in this place.
Underneath the cosmic stream,
Life unfolds like a dream.

Eternal whispers touch my heart,
In this realm, I'll play my part.
Every twinkle, a guiding hand,
Through the dark, a promise grand.

Reflections in the silent sea,
Softly shape my thoughts and me.
In the cool embrace of night,
Shining solitude feels right.

As I breathe the crisp night air,
I can sense the universe's care.
Each pulse of light a spark of hope,
Shining solitude helps me cope.

Frosty Glimmers of Forgotten Tales

Frosty glimmers in the moon's glow,
Whisper secrets only snow can know.
In the silence, echoes speak,
Of forgotten tales, unique.

With each flake that tumbles down,
History wears a silver crown.
Shadows hold the stories tight,
Guardians of the winter night.

In every drift, a tale unfolds,
Of timeless love and legends bold.
Through the frost, the past ignites,
Glimmers shining in the nights.

Wandering through this frozen land,
Feeling dreams at my command.
Every step reveals the truth,
Of forgotten joys of youth.

So let the tales of old survive,
In the cold, they come alive.
With each breath beneath the stars,
Frosty glimmers heal our scars.

Echoes of White Serenity

In the hush of winter's breath,
Snowflakes dance in silent grace,
A blanket soft, a quiet death,
Embracing earth in pale embrace.

Footsteps sink in pearly white,
Whispers linger, soft and low,
Echoes fade in fading light,
As twilight falls, the stars aglow.

Branches draped in frozen lace,
Icicles hang like crystal tears,
Nature wears a chilly face,
While peace descends and calms our fears.

Moonlight spills on fields of frost,
Illuminating night's still calm,
In this realm, there's nothing lost,
Just the magic of winter's charm.

Hearts find warmth amidst the cold,
In each sigh, a story spun,
Within the white, a beauty bold,
Whispering dreams where hope's begun.

Candlelight in the Snowfall

Flickering flames, a gentle glow,
In the dark of winter's night,
With each flake that falls so slow,
Candlelight brings warmth, soft and bright.

Gathered close, we share our tales,
Fireside laughter, sweet and near,
Outside, the stormy wind wails,
But in here, there's naught to fear.

Each candle flickers, shadows play,
As snow coats the world in white,
Moments melt and drift away,
Yet love's flame endures, our light.

A tapestry of warmth and cheer,
Against the chill that stings and bites,
In this glow, we hold so dear,
We find our peace on wintry nights.

Outside, the world is clothed in frost,
But in our hearts, the fire stays,
Through every moment, love embossed,
In candlelight, we count the days.

Brilliant Glows in the Cold

A canvas bright, the world aglow,
Underneath the silver skies,
Each breath a cloud, a frosty show,
As brilliant glimmers mesmerize.

Trees are laced in sparkling dreams,
Every branch a jeweled crown,
Nature's art through sunlight beams,
In this wonderland, we drown.

Footprints mark the silent ground,
Every step a story told,
In the quiet, magic found,
With every twinkle, moments bold.

Crystals form on window panes,
A gallery of winter's grace,
In this chill, adventure reigns,
As we explore this frozen space.

The brilliance of the cold entwines,
A frosty touch, an invitation,
In every sparkle, love defines,
Our shared hearts, a celebration.

Twinkling Hues on Frozen Ground

Underneath a sky so vast,
Stars ignite in brilliant hues,
As time drifts gently, shadows cast,
On frozen ground, a dreamy muse.

In the meadow, colors blend,
With laughter carried on the breeze,
Each twinkle seems to gently send,
A message wrapped in winter's tease.

Footsteps crunch on icy trails,
As whispers swirl in crisp, cold air,
We speak of love, our hearts unveil,
Among the twinkling, we lay bare.

A tapestry of night unfolds,
Where every twinkle holds a spark,
Through every glance, a warmth it holds,
Lighting pathways in the dark.

In this world of frozen art,
Where winter weaves its glowing song,
Each moment etched within the heart,
In twinkling hues, we all belong.

Ember of the Silent Woods

In the heart of the forest, embers glow,
Whispers of leaves in the twilight's flow.
Stars flicker softly, a silent friend,
Nature's embrace, where shadows blend.

Moonlight spills on the path so clear,
Crickets serenade, a melody near.
Branches cradle the night's soft sigh,
While time drifts gently, as moments fly.

The whispering winds tell tales of old,
Of secrets hidden, of stories told.
With every crackle, the fire ignites,
A dance of warmth on the chilly nights.

In the silence deep, the heart finds peace,
Where worries fade, and troubles cease.
Embers flicker, the warmth is shared,
In the silent woods, where love is bared.

Candle's Dance on a Snowy Eve

Upon the mantle, a candle glows,
Its warm light dances as the cold wind blows.
Frosted windows hold the winter's breath,
In this cozy haven, we forget our stress.

Outside the world wears a blanket of white,
While inside we gather, hearts alight.
Flickering shadows play on the walls,
A symphony of silence in the snow's gentle falls.

With every flick of the flame so bright,
We share our stories throughout the night.
Laughter rings out, a joyful sound,
In the glow of the candle, warmth is found.

The snowflakes whisper as they drift down,
While together we wear winter's crown.
Hand in hand, through the evening's grace,
The dance of the candle, our hearts embrace.

The Light Beneath the Snow

Beneath the cover of white so pure,
Lies a world alive, steady and sure.
Seeds of tomorrow in slumber deep,
Waiting for spring, their dreams to keep.

Each flake that tumbles, a story bestowed,
A tapestry woven upon the cold road.
Hidden treasures lie underneath,
Waiting for warmth to spark their breath.

As the sun breaks through, the icy sheen,
Reveals the whispers of what has been.
Life stirs softly in the thawing earth,
Witness to winter's quiet rebirth.

The light beneath, a promise unfolds,
In cold's embrace, the future holds.
For every barren winter's night,
There waits a bloom, ready for light.

Winter's Warmth in a Chilly Frame

Outside the window, the frost paints lace,
But inside, the hearth offers a warm embrace.
Shadows flicker as the embers spark,
In this soothing refuge, we banish the dark.

Blankets wrapped tight, we sit side by side,
As stories and laughter like rivers glide.
With every sip of cocoa, hearts ignite,
In a sanctuary built from love and delight.

The world outside may be frozen and still,
But here in our haven, we share our will.
Through chilly frames, the warmth flows bright,
Binding our spirits with soft, golden light.

As night falls gently, we hold on tight,
To moments that shimmer in winter's light.
Together we brave the cold, hand in hand,
In the warmth of our love, we firmly stand.

A Symphony of Chill and Light

Frosty whispers weave through air,
Gentle shadows dance with care.
Moonlight bathes the world in grace,
Nature's quiet, a soft embrace.

Crystals glisten, diamonds bright,
Stars awaken in the night.
Each breath mingles with the cold,
Stories of winter softly told.

Branches sway, a lullaby,
While silent flurries drift on high.
In this realm where dreams take flight,
We find our peace, a pure delight.

Echoes linger, time stands still,
Hearts are warmed by winter's chill.
A symphony of sound and light,
Guides us through the starry night.

Radiant Echoes in a Winter's Silence

In the hush of falling snow,
Quiet moments start to flow.
Nature's voice, serene and clear,
Whispers secrets for the near.

Icicles hang, a crystal show,
Reflecting warmth within the glow.
Each breath, a cloud, a fleeting wisp,
In winter's charm, we gently lisp.

Beyond the frost, a world unseen,
Radiant echoes, pure and keen.
In the stillness, hearts unite,
Breathing in the soft moonlight.

Snowflakes twirl, a dance so sweet,
Beneath our boots, a soft heartbeat.
In this silence, love ignites,
Radiant whispers, endless nights.

Starlit Lanterns Beneath the Snow

Beneath the layers, secrets lie,
Starlit lanterns in the sky.
Each flake is unique, a gentle spark,
In the stillness, they leave their mark.

Frozen branches, a work of art,
Nature's beauty, a beating heart.
Through frosty woods, we wander wide,
Hand in hand, in winter's pride.

Softly glowing, paths unfold,
Stories in whispers, quietly told.
Moonbeams cast a silver thread,
As we tread where dreams are led.

Fireplaces crackle, warmth in sight,
While outside the world embraces night.
Starlit wishes in the snow,
Guide us gently where dreams can flow.

Winter's Heart in a Warm Embrace

In winter's heart, we find our place,
A calm, serene, and warm embrace.
Fires glow with stories shared,
In the quiet, we are prepared.

Each snowy drift a blanket wide,
Holding whispers deep inside.
Under blankets, we find delight,
As shadows dance in soft twilight.

Hot cocoa sips, laughter bright,
Together facing the frosty night.
Love wraps us like a gentle shawl,
In winter's warmth, we feel it all.

Through swirling winds and coldest air,
We cherish bonds beyond compare.
Winter's heart beats strong and true,
In every moment, me and you.

Reflections of Light in a Frosty Mood

In the stillness of a frost,
Silent whispers, all seems lost.
Yet a glow begins to gleam,
Lighting up the quiet dream.

Shadows dance on icy panes,
Tales of warmth amidst the pains.
Each twinkle breaks the night's embrace,
Fleeting hope in a frozen space.

Footsteps crunch on powdered dust,
In this magic, we place our trust.
Reflections shimmer in the night,
A world alive with gentle light.

Frosty breath hangs in the air,
A canvas white, a world so rare.
Moments captured, lost in time,
Through the chill, our spirits climb.

Beyond the chill, a promise gleams,
In winter's heart, we dare to dream.
For even in a frozen world,
Warmth and wonder are unfurled.

Dreamscapes Beneath a Shimmering Sky

Beneath the stars, the dreamers lie,
In whispers soft, the night draws nigh.
A shimmering sky, a painted dome,
In this vastness, we find our home.

Waves of silver gently sway,
Guided by the moon's ballet.
Each twinkling star a tale untold,
In the night, the dreams unfold.

Clouds drift softly, shadows play,
Carrying hopes that float away.
In this realm where wishes blend,
Every moment can transcend.

Night wraps around with silken grace,
A serene path, a sacred space.
In silence, hearts begin to soar,
Dreamscapes beckon, forevermore.

With every breath, we weave our fate,
In the tapestry of the innate.
Under the shimmer, we close our eyes,
And lost in wonder, we touch the skies.

Glints of Hope Against a Frosted Backdrop

In the cold where silence reigns,
Hope ignites amidst the pains.
Tiny glints on frosted ground,
Whispers of dreams, softly found.

Each sparkling flake a wish anew,
Promises made, a bond so true.
Through the chill, we find our way,
Guided by light, through shades of gray.

Frosty breath, our fate in hand,
Together we rise, we take a stand.
Against the backdrop, stark and white,
Glimmers of hope shine through the night.

Every step, a story scribed,
In shadows deep, our hearts described.
A journey marked by trials sore,
Yet every glint opens a door.

In winter's grasp, warmth still flows,
Through every challenge, courage grows.
Frosted dreams awaken the heart,
In this cold, we find our part.

Enchanted Lanterns Amid the Snow

Lanterns glow in the midnight air,
Casting light with tender care.
Amidst the snow, they softly sway,
Guiding wanderers on their way.

Whispers of stories in the night,
Every flicker, a pulse of light.
In this winter's enchanted embrace,
Magic resides in every space.

Footprints lost in the snowy deep,
Echoes of dreams we hold and keep.
Under the lanterns' gentle gleam,
Hearts awaken, igniting a dream.

A dance of shadows, a magical sight,
In the stillness, the world feels right.
Amidst the snow, time stands still,
As lanterns weave their wondrous thrill.

In quiet moments, we find the glow,
Reviving spirits, casting off woe.
Enchanted nights bring forth our song,
In the light, we all belong.

Traces of Warmth in the Cold

Upon the snow, soft footprints lie,
Echoes of laughter drift and sigh.
A candle flickers in the still night air,
In this chilly world, warmth is rare.

Embers glow, the hearth's embrace,
Whispers of joy in a quiet space.
Fingers entwined beneath thick blankets,
Hearts beat together, love never franks.

While frost adorns each windowpane,
Memories dance like a gentle flame.
Come closer, my dear, warm me whole,
In traces of warmth, we find our soul.

Winter's breath sings a gentle tune,
Stars shimmer bright like a silver moon.
Let our hearts thaw under snowflakes' fall,
In the cold night air, we still stand tall.

Against the chill, your smile ignites,
A beacon of hope on the longest nights.
Traces of warmth in the icy fold,
Together we'll shine, our story told.

Radiant Serenity of Winter's Heart

In the hush of snow, peace unwinds,
Nature's serenity, its beauty binds.
Crystal branches stretch with grace,
In winter's heart, we find our place.

Silent streets draped in white,
With stars above, a soft, warm light.
Footprints leading to love's sweet door,
Radiant serenity, forevermore.

Chill in the air, but warmth inside,
Under covers, where dreams abide.
The world outside may seem so stark,
Yet in our hearts, a glowing spark.

Softly falling, the flakes descend,
Each one a gem that the skies send.
Wrapped in comfort, we share our glee,
Winter's heart beats just for thee.

With every breath, the frost exhales,
A tranquil calm as night prevails.
Radiant moments, cherished and true,
In winter's heart, I find you too.

Whispers in the Winter Glow

Beneath the stars, the snowflakes swirl,
Magic weaves in the nighttime whirl.
A fire crackles, stories shared,
In the winter glow, we are ensnared.

Whispers dance with the gentle breeze,
Timeless secrets among the trees.
Frosty air filled with tender sighs,
As moonlight bathes all in sweet surprise.

The world is hushed in still delight,
Embracing warmth on this cold night.
Your laughter twinkles like distant stars,
As we dream together, without any bars.

In every flake, a tale unfolds,
Of ancient nights and love that holds.
Whispers echo, hearts aligned,
In winter's glow, true love we find.

Let us wander where the shadows lay,
Finding joy in this tender play.
In the chill, our spirits flow,
Forever bound in winter's glow.

Frost-kissed Illumination

Glistening frost paints the dawn bright,
Nature awakens in beautiful light.
Every crystal a delicate lace,
Frost-kissed wonders, a gentle embrace.

Morning whispers through the trees,
A symphony sung with the softest breeze.
Each breath frosty, a vapor's dance,
In this tranquil world, we find our chance.

Illuminated paths, sparkling white,
Every step leads to pure delight.
With you beside me, the chill fades, drama,
Frost-kissed moments, a treasured panorama.

Winter's beauty is fragile and rare,
With every laugh, our love's repair.
Under the sun, the frost softly glows,
Together, our warmth against the cold flows.

Hold my hand as we journey on,
In this frosted wonder, fears are gone.
Frost-kissed illumination stays,
In our hearts, forever blaze.

Ethereal Light in a Winter's Veil

In a world of snow and ice,
Soft whispers fill the air,
Moonlight dances on the ground,
A shimmering, silver glare.

Frosted branches glisten bright,
As shadows gently creep,
Night wraps us in its embrace,
While the world is fast asleep.

Stars twinkle like tiny gems,
Adorning a velvet sky,
Ethereal light surrounds us,
As winter's breath drifts by.

Each flake a silent story,
Falling without a sound,
We walk beneath the glow,
In this magic we have found.

A wonderland of dreams revealed,
In every icy breath,
Together we find solace,
In the beauty of this quest.

Celestial Radiance on Icy Paths

The moon hangs high above,
Casting shadows deep and wide,
On paths where frost has settled,
In the hush of winter's pride.

Celestial radiance glows,
Guiding us through the night,
Steps crunching underfoot,
In the soft and silver light.

Whispers of the starry skies,
Echo through the frosty air,
Each moment holds a secret,
Wrapped in glittering flair.

The chill bites at our cheeks,
Yet warmth is found inside,
As we walk these icy paths,
With nature as our guide.

Here among the starlit dreams,
Our worries fade away,
In the magic of the night,
As we let our hearts sway.

The Warmth Within the Chill

Beneath the blanket of the night,
As frost adorns each pane,
There's a warmth within the chill,
That kindles love's sweet flame.

Crisp air fills our every breath,
While laughter twirls and spins,
In the glow of flickering lights,
Where every joy begins.

Hands clasped tight against the cold,
Hearts beating soft and true,
In the shadow of the moon,
We find warmth in all we do.

Snowflakes whirl like fleeting dreams,
As whispers float and twine,
In the midst of winter's frost,
We find the love divine.

So let the chill wrap 'round us,
As we dance beneath the sky,
For in this heated moment,
Our spirits learn to fly.

Shimmering Lanterns in the Dark

In the midst of winter's night,
Lanterns glow like fireflies,
Guiding footsteps through the gloom,
Beneath the vast, starry skies.

Each flicker tells a story,
Of warmth and hope anew,
As we wander through the dark,
With dreams both bright and true.

Shadows dance around us,
In the stillness of the air,
While shimmering lights surround us,
A reminder that we care.

So let our hearts be lanterns,
In the world that seems so stark,
For together we find light,
In the beauty of the dark.

With every step in silence,
In the glow we stake our claim,
Shimmering lanterns guide the way,
Through life's sweet, gentle flame.

Illumination Beneath the Stars

In the hush of the night, they gleam,
Whispers of light from a distant dream.
Each twinkle a story, a heart laid bare,
Guiding lost souls through the darkened air.

A canvas of velvet, softly unfurled,
Dancing with secrets from another world.
The moon's gentle glow casts shadows near,
Illuminating paths we hold dear.

Stars weave their magic, a shimmering thread,
Connecting our thoughts, what's left unsaid.
In radiant silence, we find our place,
As starlight carves memories into space.

Such beauty above, a celestial show,
Encouraging dreams like a river to flow.
Under this blanket, we're one with the night,
Embracing the wonder, the deep cosmic light.

To gaze at the heavens, so vast and wide,
In the illumination, let hope be our guide.
For beneath the stars, we are never alone,
In the universe's heart, we find our home.

Embracing the Chilly Glow

When winter descends with a crystalline breath,
The air turns sharp, a dance with death.
Frost-kissed whispers creep in the night,
Yet there's warmth within the chilly light.

Sparks from the hearth flicker and spring,
As shadows grow long, love takes wing.
We gather close 'round the glowing fire,
Sharing our dreams, our hearts' desire.

With each gust of wind that rattles the pane,
We find solace in stories to ease the strain.
For in this cold, there lies a warmth,
A bond that flourishes, a gentle storm.

Moonlight spills softly on snow's pure face,
Painting the world in a silvery lace.
Embracing the night, we find our song,
In the chilly glow where we belong.

Though frost may bite, our spirits rise,
Under the blanket of midnight skies.
In this tranquil moment of wonder and peace,
Our laughter and love will never cease.

Luminescent Silence

In the still of the dawn, a soft light creeps,
Through glassy horizons, the daylight leaps.
Silence envelops the waking earth,
A quiet embrace, a moment of mirth.

The shadows recede, giving way to gold,
Stories of life in the glow unfold.
Each ray a soft hand, a gentle caress,
Illuminating dreams none can suppress.

In this hushed moment, clarity reigns,
As whispers of light break through the chains.
The world feels anew, fresh in its grace,
In the luminescent silence, we find our place.

Time stretches onward, ethereal and sweet,
While nature awakes on soft, silent feet.
With hearts light as feathers, we dare to believe,
In the beauty of life that we freely receive.

As day blooms around us, we open our eyes,
Grasping the magic that underlies skies.
In this stillness, a promise unfolds,
In the luminescent quiet, our spirits are bold.

Frosted Flicker of Hope

Amidst the frost on a winter's morn,
A flicker emerges, though weathered and worn.
Each crystal shining holds stories untold,
A testament woven, both fragile and bold.

In the chill of the air, dreams seem to freeze,
Yet hope's tender light rides on every breeze.
Beneath layers of ice, life stirs with a sigh,
Waiting for warmth from a sun drawing nigh.

The world may be quiet, the branches may sway,
Yet within the stillness, we carve out our way.
With every soft heartbeat, we refuse to despair,
For the frosted flicker is always there.

In shadows of winter, we nurture our flame,
Finding beauty in struggle, we rise without shame.
For hope is a whisper, a glimmering spark,
Lighting our path when we wander in dark.

So, gather your dreams like snowflakes that fall,
Let their beauty surround you, embracing them all.
For in each frosted moment, may we learn to cope,
Wrapped in the warmth of this flicker of hope.

Threads of Light in the Snowbound Night

In the silence, shadows dance,
Whispers weave in twilight's trance.
Stars above like pearls aglow,
Threading dreams in soft white snow.

Footsteps crisp on frosty ground,
Snowflakes gentle, wrapped around.
Moonlight spills on frozen streams,
Lighting paths of quiet dreams.

Every shimmer, a silent song,
Echoes of where souls belong.
Nature's quilt, a soft embrace,
In the night, we find our place.

Glistening under the night sky,
Silver ribbons, floating high.
A tapestry of peace and light,
Guiding hearts through snowy night.

As the world holds its breath tight,
Threads of love ignite the night.
In this stillness, we take flight,
Carried home on wings of light.

Frosted Feelings and Glowing Dreams

In the morning, the world is bright,
Frosted feelings in the light.
Whispers of warmth in the cold,
Stories of love waiting to unfold.

Icy branches, sparkles gleam,
Heartfelt wishes in a dream.
Crisp air carries hopes anew,
As winter's magic starts to brew.

Glimmers caught in every breath,
Moments cherished, defying death.
Glowing embers in the heart,
Frosted feelings set apart.

Footprints left on shimmering ground,
Echoes of laughter softly sound.
With every step, we find our way,
Glowing dreams guide us each day.

In the dusk, horizons blend,
As frosted feelings never end.
Under stars, our spirits soar,
In glowing dreams, we are evermore.

Flickering Echoes on Icy Slopes

On icy slopes where shadows play,
Flickering echoes light the way.
Chill winds carrying tales untold,
In hushed whispers, spirits bold.

Footsteps crunching with each stride,
In the twilight, we abide.
Glowing fires on distant peaks,
Warmth found in the silence it speaks.

Snowflakes swirling, a soft ballet,
Inviting dreams where hearts can stay.
Fragrant pine and whispers clear,
Nature beckons, drawing near.

Every flicker, a memory bright,
Shadows soften in the night.
With each turn, a tale unfolds,
In icy depths, our journey holds.

As the stars begin to gleam,
We chase the echoes of our dream.
Flickering lights weave through the dark,
Guiding us as we embark.

A Web of Light in the Winter's Grasp

In winter's hold, a web of light,
Woven softly through the night.
Glistening threads in the frost's embrace,
Illuminating time and space.

Whispers linger in the air,
Echoes of love, everywhere.
Each glimmer, a promise made,
In the silence, dreams cascade.

Cold moon rises, shadows blend,
Hidden paths around the bend.
Stars above like silver lace,
In the night, we find our place.

With every heartbeat, warmth is near,
A web of light that calms our fears.
In the depths of winter's chill,
Hope ignites with every thrill.

As dawn breaks, colors bloom,
Dancing light chases away gloom.
In this web, we find our peace,
A winter's grasp that grants release.

Crystal Glows of Memory

In the quiet corners of the mind,
Whispers of laughter gently unwind.
Fragrant echoes of days long past,
Moments like jewels, forever to last.

Flickers of light dance through the haze,
Each shard reflects a sunbeam's gaze.
Time casts shadows, yet still they shine,
Embracing the warmth, the heart enshrined.

Nostalgic tunes that softly play,
Woven threads of yesterday.
Each luminescent piece we hold,
A tapestry rich, a story told.

Beneath the layers of fleeting years,
The crystal glows chase away fears.
Holding onto the joy and pain,
In their brilliance, love shall remain.

So we gather, those memories bold,
In the tapestry, each hand we hold.
Crystal glows that light the way,
Guiding us through night and day.

Celestial Embrace of a Winter's Night

Stars twinkle softly in the dark,
As snowflakes fall, they leave their mark.
The world's serene in a silver cloak,
Beneath the sky, naught but a cloak.

Moonlight spills like liquid grace,
Illuminating each quiet space.
Breath of winter, crisp and clear,
In this embrace, all is near.

Frosty whispers weave through the trees,
A lullaby carried by the breeze.
Wonders await in the stillness found,
In this moment, magic is crowned.

Footprints trace the path of dreams,
In the hush where silence gleams.
A tapestry of night unfolds,
In celestial arms, the heart beholds.

The chill wraps close, a tender tie,
Beneath the vast, unyielding sky.
In winter's night, a truth ignites,
Love shines bright in tranquil sights.

Shadows Under a Frosted Sky

Morning breaks through a silver veil,
While shadows dance and wail.
Frosted air clings to the chill,
Nature's pulse keeps time still.

Branches shimmer, dressed in white,
Whispers echo in the light.
Each step crunched on snow below,
In the silence, stories flow.

Chilled winds carry soft refrains,
Tales of joy, remnants of pains.
Under the frosted sky we roam,
Here in shadows, we find home.

Glimmers spark in the soft twilight,
Tender hearts embrace the night.
Here we stand, intertwined and free,
In every shadow, a memory.

In this realm where stillness sighs,
Crafted dreams that never die.
Shadows cradle all we've sought,
Under a sky where love is wrought.

Dawn's Light on the Snowy Verge

As dawn ignites the frozen ground,
A golden glow awakens sound.
Snowflakes dance in morning's rays,
A promise held in soft displays.

Glistening whispers greet the day,
Painting paths of bright array.
Each moment glows like porcelain,
A fresh start wrapped in soft refrain.

Tidings borne on playful winds,
Echoing where the silence ends.
Life emerges from slumber's dream,
In dawn's embrace, all's as it seems.

Footprints print the snowy edge,
Marking paths, we gently hedge.
With hope renewed and spirits high,
We chase the light beneath the sky.

Together we sing, hearts entwined,
In a world where love is blind.
Dawn's light whispers to the verge,
In its grace, we find the urge.

A Dance of Light in the Cold

In shadows deep, the stars ignite,
They twinkle softly, pure and bright.
Each flicker sings a tale untold,
A dance of light in the cold.

Winter's breath drapes every tree,
With silver frost, a sight to see.
A gentle hush wraps all around,
As whispers of the night abound.

The moon at play, a golden hue,
It paints the world in dreamy view.
With every step, the crunch of snow,
A symphony where soft winds blow.

In frosty fields, the silence reigns,
While magic flows through chilled veins.
Together we span the icy air,
In the light's embrace, free of care.

Nature's art in winter's glow,
A canvas vast with brilliant show.
Each moment shared, a story spun,
In the dance of light, we become one.

Silvery Hues Against the Night Sky

The sky unfurls, a velvet seam,
With silvery hues that softly gleam.
Each star a wish, a secret told,
A map of dreams in night's sweet hold.

Clouds drift lazily, soft and white,
Painting the canvas of the night.
The calmest whisper, an elegant sigh,
As the world below feels time pass by.

Reflections dance on waters deep,
Where moonlit ripples serenely leap.
The cool embrace of evening's kiss,
In this moment, purest bliss.

A symphony of light takes flight,
Illuminating the heart's delight.
Each twinkle beckons, a gentle nudge,
Awakening hopes that never budge.

In the stillness, dreams arise,
As endless stars claim the sky.
Silvery hues' enchanting play,
Guide us through the night to day.

Glow of the Whispering Pines

Among the pines, a gentle breeze,
Carries whispers through the trees.
The moonlight drapes each bough and pine,
In their embrace, our hearts align.

A glow emerges, soft and warm,
A refuge safe from every storm.
Beneath the branches, shadows fall,
Where nature's spirit beckons all.

The scent of earth, a fragrant kiss,
Awakens senses lost in bliss.
Each rustle tells a tale so grand,
In the woodland's quiet, hand in hand.

Stars above in velvet dark,
Illuminate the forest's spark.
A symphony of night unfolds,
As nature's magic gently holds.

Together, wrapped in pine's soft sway,
We linger in the dance of play.
In every murmur, every sigh,
The glow of love will never die.

Kindling Hope in the Winter Nights

The winter nights, so cold and clear,
Whisper dreams we long to hear.
With every star that lights the fray,
Kindling hope for a brighter day.

Fires flicker with a gentle glow,
Casting warmth on the world below.
In the crackling sound, we find our way,
Through darkest nights to the dawn of day.

The air is crisp, the silence deep,
Beneath the stars, the world will sleep.
Yet in our hearts, a flame still glows,
For every ending, a new hope grows.

Together we spark a shared delight,
In stories told through the quiet night.
With every laugh, our spirits soar,
In the warmth of love that we hold dear.

As frost may settle on the ground,
In every heartbeat, hope is found.
Kindling dreams through winter's chill,
With love as our guide, we climb the hill.

www.ingramcontent.com/pod-product-compliance
Ingram Content Group UK Ltd.
Pitfield, Milton Keynes, MK11 3LW, UK
UKHW032223171224
452550UK00006B/76